LETTERS *from the* WILDERNESS *of* MODERN PARENTING

Written by **VASHTI SUMMERVILL**

Illustrated by **WENDY BLICKENSTAFF**

ISBN(paperback) 979-8-9895819-0-0
ISBN (ebook) 979-8-9895819-1-7

Published by:

SHOWING UP BETTER

www.showingupbetter.com

CONTENTS

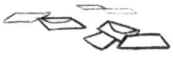

FORWARD
by the Author

This book is a collection of things I have learned on my own profound parenting and professional journeys. The letters are written in first person as if they are direct communications between a parent and a child. Some of the letters may apply directly to your parenting experiences, and some may not. My hope is that this book will provide you with a fresh perspective and new tools.

These passages are meant to be concise and easy to digest. Read it cover to cover or just flip to a page or image that might give you the nourishment you are needing in this moment. Perhaps there will be a page that captures something you are wanting to express to your child and you can share it with them and begin a productive conversation.

I started my parenting journey with very few tools. I took a birthing class and learned the basics about how to keep a baby alive. As my children grew into unique individuals and discovered the power of free will, the struggles began. The relationships became strained and our journey often felt arduous and painful.

As my kids grew bigger, so did the problems we faced. My responses became more ineffective. The world got faster, sadder, and more challenging. I was not prepared to meet any of this. I felt helpless.

It's a hard time to grow up. The challenges our kids face are very different from those we faced just thirty or forty years ago - or even five years ago. Dr. John Duffy says that we must become students of our children's world because it is changing so fast—it is not the same one we grew up in. We as parents are navigating a "wild west," facing challenges past generations have not faced.

The period of adolescence seems to be longer. It might start around age nine or ten, and can often go into the late twenties. We are in for the long haul.

There is so much mystery in this human experience. We know very little about how we are hard-wired and why some people experience mental health challenges and others do not. Most of us know so little about how to navigate our own difficult emotions and even less about how to help others. Relationships with others can be fraught with misunderstanding, hurt feelings, and a variety of challenges—especially the parent-child relationship.

Did I mention that the world we live in has gotten faster, sadder, and more challenging? These conditions have made the nearly empty toolbox we entered the parenting journey with even more inadequate.

Kids come with a variety of unique talents and challenges. I believe that many of the thoughts in this book are universal, but I also know that some of you have been gifted with kids with challenges not everyone faces—everything from autism to severe mental illness. While these perspectives won't solve all challenges, I hope that somewhere in this book is at least one thing that will ease your burden and move you forward in a positive way.

I work with brave parents going through unimaginable experiences with kids who are depressed, anxious, have experienced severe trauma, are thinking about or have tried to end their life, are deep into extreme substance abuse, or with whom their relationships seem fractured beyond repair. Sometimes, what is needed is to cut through the noise and the overwhelm by simply asking, "What does this moment require of me?"

We are hard on ourselves. A lot of shame, guilt, and regret accompanies us on this parenting journey. I am working to be more gentle with myself and I hope you will too. Your decision to read this book affirms that you care about your role as a parent. You are still trying. I don't want to evaluate my parenting based on the mistakes I have made, but instead focus on the repairs, the course corrections, the willingness to learn, and the fact that I wake up each morning, roll up my sleeves and show up, no matter how hard it is. Don't let perfect be the enemy of showing up, learning, repairing, and loving.

As mentioned, modern parenting presents some very unique challenges. No one needs another "how to" book. There is no method or technique that will suddenly change everything about our parenting and our relationship with our kids. The parent/child journey is a messy and winding road. Most relationships are.

The first step is to accept that it will always be messy and then embrace the mess as an amazing laboratory for learning more about our own humanity and the unique children we have been gifted with.

The next step is to replace our inner voice, which might be one of shaming and regret, with a voice filled with some loving kindness towards ourself. As the saying goes, most of us are doing the best we can with the tools we have.

I often tell my kids that I am working hard to own my mistakes, to learn every day, and to keep showing up to do the hard work of growing myself and my relationships. By picking up a book like this, you are doing just that.

In addition to being kinder to ourselves, it is important to assume that beneath all the struggle, there is deep and innate goodness within our children. While not easy, we can work through our exhaustion, anger, and really stuck places with our kids by trying to reframe situations and look through fresh eyes. When we look through a lens of empathy and curiosity and build our perspective-shifting muscles, we are modeling something powerful for our kids.

Even though this is my work, I am in the big, messy, beautiful boat with you. I will continue to ride the waves with as much humility and grace as I can muster. And I will be cheering for you at the same time.

Vashti Summervill
Family Healing Pathways
December 2023

FORWARD

by the Illustrator

I describe myself as a community-builder artist, printmaker, parent, activity therapist, behavior interventionist, student, and teacher. I have known Vashti Summervill for over ten years through her community work and coaching practice. When I was looking for someone to partner with to create a mental health book, Vashti and I met for coffee, and the idea for this book organically materialized. We both have a lot to share about our work with adolescents and young adults and their families. Some of the information in this book has been acquired through painful personal struggles, while other parts are derived from professional experience. It has been a pleasure to collaborate with Vashti on this project.

I am a practicing artist and operate a business focused on printmaking with visual themes related to mental health. Through my work, I see teens struggling with learning disabilities and mental health problems. I teach them coping skills and provide a creative outlet for them to express themselves. Art is communication, and through art, adolescents learn new ways to communicate, new skills through which they can connect with others. I hope the images I have created for this book help parents and adolescents to fully unpack the written concepts.

Our early experiences can significantly impact who we become as a person. Most adults remember when they were adolescents, including rehearsed narratives of their life from that period. Some of these stories are fun and adventurous, like something from a sitcom, while others are much darker and more painful. My teenage stories are filled with the highs of sports, friends, and mischief, and the lows of a reading disability, relationship heartaches, and family dynamics.

My reading disability led me to art. Art was the one area in my life where I was on an even playing field with other people. It is my first language and my best communication skill. I've spent my life using art to help people connect. It helps me and others understand the world more creatively. It can facilitate deep healing and meaningful discussions in unexpected ways.

The pieces I made for this book are linoleum block prints. I thought long and hard about how to synergize my images with Vashti's writing and add constructive new ideas and concepts. The prints address the subject matter of the writing in minimal silhouette shapes. The images are open-ended to allow readers to explore their own ideas and associations based on their lived experience, without the constraints of too many visual cues like clothes, hair, skin color, body type, or gender. I try to avoid cluttering the subject matter with unnecessary information.

As we began working on this book, Vashti and I had some key goals in mind. We wanted to create a judgment-free zone where teens, young adults, and adults can begin productive and effective conversations. We also wanted to create some "aha!" moments to inspire people to treat one another with grace and humility, and help people agree to disagree gracefully if no middle ground can be reached. I believe that we have achieved our goals. I hope that our readers feel the same and that this book provides some relief from suffering and enables them to find creative ways to set boundaries and love one another.

Wendy Blickenstaff
Blick-Studios LLC
December 2023

*These letters are a fictional
amalgamation of personal, professional,
and cultural experiences and observations—
situations that are relatable and real
for countless parents and children.*

THE MIRACLE *of* YOU

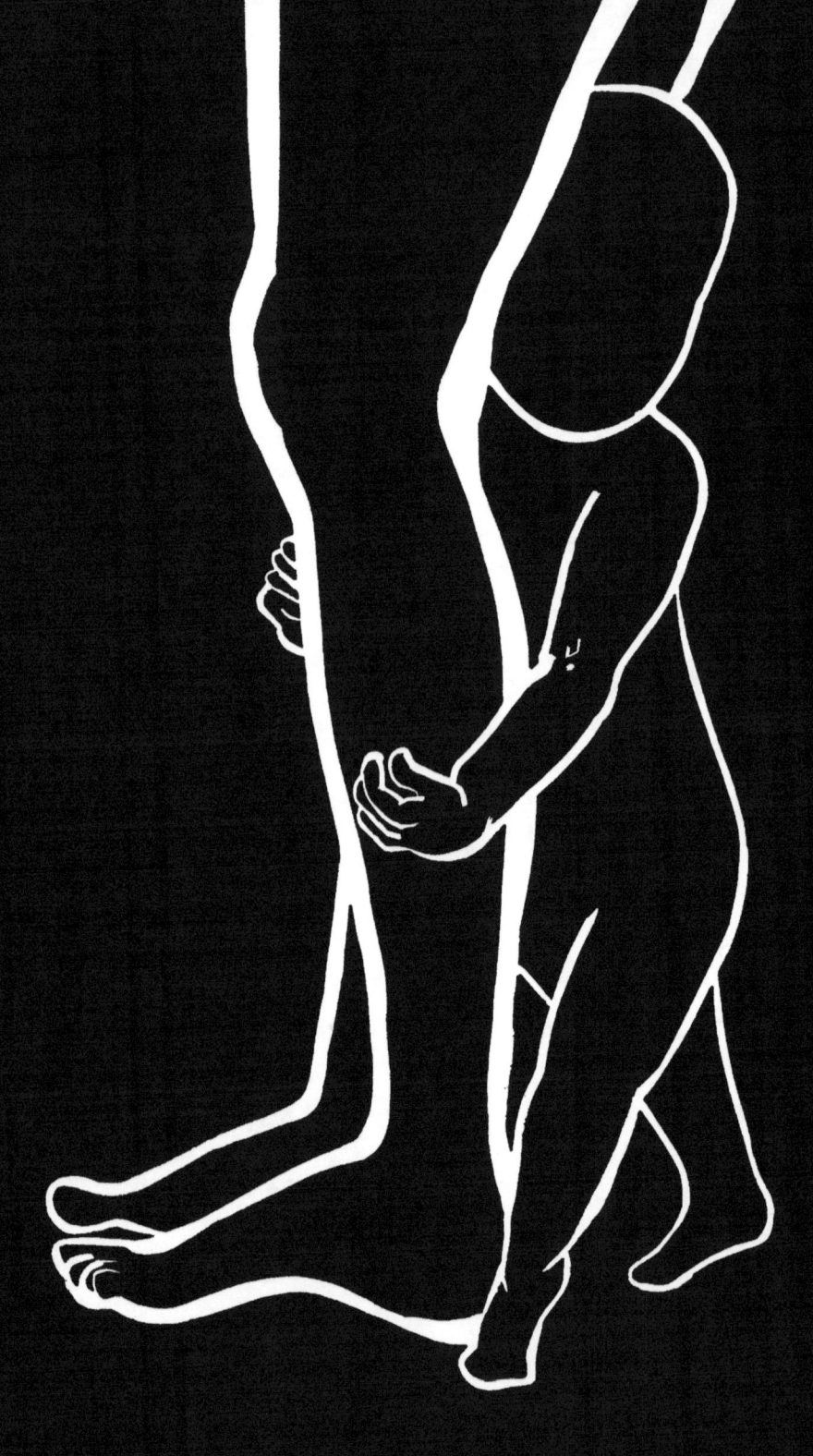

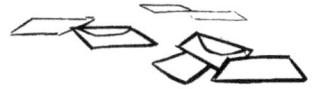

S omeone taught me a great technique for when you are really under my skin with all your teenage teenagery.

They told me that when the going gets tough, it helps to look at photos of your children when they were little.

I really like this idea.

I look at photos of you as a toddler with chubby cheeks, naked in the summer grass, holding a hose as you ask your sister to spray your bum off because you decided it was an excellent idea to poo in the front yard.

I look at you learning to ride a bike or sliding down our stairs on a window seat cushion wearing a bicycle helmet.

I find the photo of you with a little chair strapped to your back, standing on the front sidewalk. It was your jet pack that you said would take you back to Disneyland.

I find photos of you with pets and grandparents and crazy cousin gatherings.

I find photos of the first days of school and photos of you with no front teeth. Pictures of Halloween costumes and you playing with the contents of the "dress-up box," which you used to do for hours.

I find old videos of you singing and dancing with abandon—pure personality. Your personality. A personality like no one else because you are your own unique miracle.

I am reminded of the magical, mysterious miracle that is you and I marvel. Yes, I like this. I plan to marvel at the miracle of you much more often.

VALEDICTORIAN *of* EMPATHY

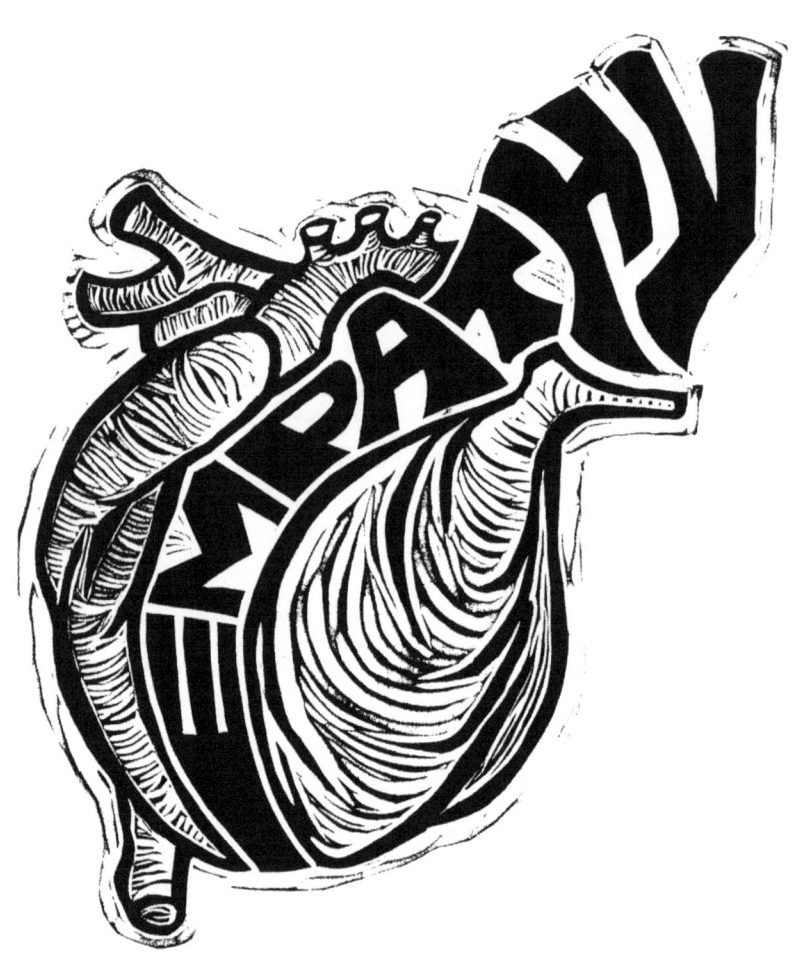

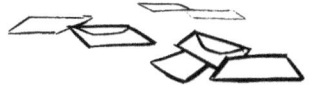

I wish for you your very own kind of success.

I'm not talking about making more money than your parents, or prestige, or buying a bigger house, or having better things. You see right through that anyway. You are dreaming a new dream.

I would like to know more about your dream. I would like to know how you define success for yourself. I don't think I have asked you enough questions like this because I have been too busy asking you to clean your room or unload the dishwasher.

You never fit into the traditional school box. You call BS on the linear college path. I can't blame you. Times have changed. I think you view the transition into adulthood differently than I was programmed to. You think for yourself in ways I never did. I probably haven't told you this, but that is pretty badass.

When school sometimes felt like torture to you, perhaps you were getting a message from your higher self. You have a deep knowing about what feels right (and wrong) for you, and you are trying to let that guide you and blaze your own trail.

You could see that you were being taught more math than you needed, and not enough about how to focus on what counts.

You questioned the status quo. "Where are the classes on communication, relationships, resilience, and neuroscience?"

You always could find the person who looked lonely and start a conversation or offer a kind word at just the right moment.

Sometimes your one-liners still catch me off guard and give me the belly laugh medicine I need.

Your scales have naturally always seemed to tip towards a sense of justice. You have an open-heartedness and non-judgmental nature towards all that is living. How you treat people and animals and insects leaves me in awe.

I always said that if there were a valedictorian of empathy, compassion, humor, or wit, you would have been on that award podium.

GRIEVING QUESTIONS

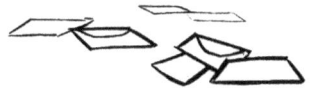

I am grieving.

I feel tired and bruised, defeated, lost.

Why are you so depressed? Where does all your anxiety come from?

Why do you cut yourself? Why do you self-medicate so much?

Why do you want to kill yourself?

Where are your grit and perseverance?

I feel confused. I tried. I really did. I've invested everything I have in you. I did my best to give you a really good and stable life.

I feel sad. I made mistakes. I own them. I really do. I can see some things more clearly now.

I have regrets. I would definitely do some things differently. I know that sometimes I made things worse.

I feel angry. Angry at a world that seems out of control.

I feel angry at you sometimes. Why can't you try harder? I have done lots of heavy lifting for you. When will you start to work just as hard on your own behalf?

In many ways, your life and childhood seem much easier than mine.

Why are you so mean to me sometimes? I feel like I can't take any more arrows from you. I am at a loss.

I am lost.

Then again, I do not know your internal experience.

I feel curious. What is it like to live as you, inside your head and body?

Why are you so stuck? Why are we stuck?

I find myself wondering what happened to the nostalgic ways I remember childhood. My teen years were definitely angsty but I also found a lot of wonder, magic, and excitement for what was directly in front of me and the future paths not yet taken.

I feel sorry for myself. I don't want to, but I feel like a victim. Why were we born into this time and culture to raise kids? Does every generation feel this way? This feels worse. Culture and society have shaped the sharp and difficult journey we are on but what are culture and society? It is a quilt made of all of us and I have to own some of the pieces I have stitched in. This also gives me hope and helps me feel like I have some choice and control in making things better.

I try to relate and tell you that I do remember some of the hard parts of being a teen. You tell me it's worse. You tell me that my generation has ruined the world. You tell me that I don't understand what it is like to grow up today. You are correct. I don't.

This also means that I have often been at a loss as to how to parent in this world.

This grief is real. But so is my hope.

MAGICAL THINKING INSTEAD *of* MUSCLE MEMORY

My abs may not be toned but my muscle memory of being in a fear state or a mindset of "something must always be wrong" is rock hard.

I want to train new muscles. I would like to strengthen my magical thinking muscles.

I don't want to let the tasks of daily life or the steady stream of bad news distract me from the miracles and beauty that still exist.

I'm not saying positive thinking will cure all that is wrong in the world. I'm just saying that both things are true. There is suffering AND there are miracles and magic everywhere.

My thoughts trick me into believing more things are wrong than actually are. I catch myself scanning for problems and, for some strange reason, wanting to pick fights with family members over nothing. I can be such a weirdo.

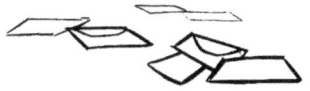

Nothing is black and white except the fact that nothing is black and white. In our very polarized world, it often seems that there are only two options. You're either for something or against it. You are on Team A or Team B. There is a right way and a wrong way. I don't have to look further than inside myself to know that this is not true. I am complicated.

I do good things and I do crappy things. That doesn't make me all saint or all sinner. I am complicated.

Did you know that the original word in the Bible that has been translated as "sin" actually means "to miss the mark?" Missing the mark means I get to try again. This conjures images of learning to ride my banana-seat bike, falling, then trying again and again until I could cruise on down the road.

I like this image of being a "mark-misser" as opposed to a scary "sinner" who is going to burn in the hot place. In reality, the hottest place is probably just inside my head. But the truth is, as a parent and as a person, I am a prolific sinner, aka, "mark-misser."

I am complicated. Sometimes I can "pitch a fit" just like a teen or a toddler. I am not proud of my fit-pitching. When it happens, it feels like a switch has flipped. It feels involuntary. My nervous system gets suddenly agitated. In part, it's just a really bad habit and a skill deficit. I have a hard time expressing myself when I feel misunderstood.

I often feel misunderstood and under-appreciated as a mother and as a wife.

I'm also quick to judge. I have selfish tendencies. I know that I, in turn, under-appreciate my family. I could definitely work on cultivating more gratitude.

I'm going to say I "pitch a fit" somewhere between six to twelve times per year. Each time I find myself doing this, I say I will stop myself the next time before it happens, practice what I preach, take a pause, etc. But it's hard to implement.

My fit-pitching comes in the form of angry, passive-aggressive, sarcastic phrases such as…

- "That's right! I'm the worst mom ever. How sad for you that you didn't get a better mom."

- "I'm such a #$$%^ #$%^!!!!!"

- "Maybe I will just disappear and your life will be better!"

This is usually followed by your response that goes something like (cue eye rolling)…

- "Here it is."

- "You make it all about you."

- "Here we go again."

- "You always do this."

Let's look at my latest episode. We had just ended a wonderful vacation. We were having a family lunch before we parted ways—you returning to work and school and us returning home. Right before lunch, I saw a couple of vape cartridges in your car. It triggered me. I am so sick of worrying about substance use. Historically, I have reason to worry, but I do acknowledge that I am a scorekeeper and have a hard time changing the story in my head.

On the one hand, I know that you are aware of what is healthy and what is not, and I see you trying to make different choices. On the other hand, I can't even count how many times I have seen the remnants of some sort of substance in your room or car and your response has been, "That's a friend's" or "That's really old." My favorite was when you tried to tell me a vape was a pedometer. I believed you for a second, but then I remembered that at that time, you didn't take walks.

We sat down to lunch (and I was already annoyed by the vape cartridges), and I asked your sibling a question about plans for the coming week off of school. He said he had an appointment to get his hair died. I replied (with a heavy dose of snark), "With what money?"

My feelings are complicated. We are still paying for the majority of both of your lives. When you spend some of your money on alcohol, nicotine, or marijuana, it feels disrespectful and bothers me. It feels like we are inadvertently paying for these things when you seem to have extra money to pay for other luxuries like dying your hair. Maybe I shouldn't have gotten upset about him getting his hair done. What harm is there in giving yourself a little boost of self-esteem and joy as you continue to navigate a tough world?

I want you to know that I actually find you to be more grateful, conscientious, and generous than entitled. You ask before renting a movie on our Amazon account. You give a little money to a friend or stranger's Go Fund Me when you see that someone is suffering. You care about paying back money you have borrowed. You write your grandparents thank you cards and check in with them often. You want to work and have always been an employee with integrity. You are actually pretty awesome.

I love how during this fit, you said, "I can't remember which brain is the bad brain—upstairs or downstairs? Which brain are you in, Mom?"

Boom! My switch was flipped, and I was solidly in downstairs brain. Ugh! But my ego… my pride, would not let me admit that the size of my reaction was overblown in proportion to what was going on. It's not easy to bring oneself out of a fit. I appreciate that you coached me in that moment, even though my ego kept me in a "mad martyr state."

I come from a line of fit-pitchers and martyrs. Genetic habit, I guess. Perhaps you will evolve beyond this.

I coach that behavior is always a message. Looking back at when my mom pitched similar fits, I wonder in what ways she was feeling misunderstood, unappreciated, and stressed. I wish I had known about this principle then and been able to think about her that way—it would have helped me and would have been a loving thing I could have done for her. I think you do this for me more than I did for my own mom.

I know that at this particular moment, I was feeling stressed about transitions. Dad and I were both making career changes. I was having a hard time being flexible in my thinking and sitting in the discomfort and uncertainty of being in between.

You both have transitions coming up too, and I feel uncertain about what the future holds for you. I'm a planner and like to map things out. But at this point in my life, I know that things don't go according to plan. I know that one of life's biggest lessons is to learn to sit in uncertainty. I also need to replace doubt or mistrust in your abilities with confidence in you. You are wise, resilient, and capable. Much more so than I was at your age.

You are also in tune with our current life transition. When we were on a walk, you were inviting me to dream about new possibilities the way you are dreaming about new possibilities. My mom worry is never lost on you. I think I'm hiding it but I'm not. You have been kindly inviting me to release it. You said, "Take me off the roster, Coach." It was compassionate. I believe it was your way of saying two things to me: "Dream big and live your life," and, "Stop worrying about me. I got this."

One last thought on a possible underlying current as I pitched this fit. I was probably just sad that our time together was coming to an end. I am still trying to make sense of empty nesting, new chapters ahead, aging and the passage of time.

I am complicated. I am trying to breathe through it all, be in the moment, and trust that things work out. They always do. We have always been taken care of.

I pitch a fit. I apologize. You offer me grace. We talk about ways to improve communication. We rebound. I am really grateful for the grace that you give me. I am working at offering you grace whenever I can.

I also know that I have done lots of good stuff. I'm going to hold my head high for that. I'm going to work on forgiving myself for my mistakes and missteps. The crappy doesn't cancel the good but the good doesn't cancel the crappy. It's just all part of the gig of being human. It's complicated.

I'm going to try extra hard to acknowledge all the amazing parts of those closest to me and forgive their mistakes and missteps too.

I think this all starts with me just acknowledging that I am messy. Being human is messy.

One of my favorite quotes comes from a book by Fredrik Backman, called, *My Grandmother Asked Me to Tell You She's Sorry*:

"Granny then said the real trick of life was that almost no one is entirely a shit and almost no one is entirely not a shit. The hard part of life is keeping as much on the not-a-shit side as one can."

I vow to work on keeping on the not-a-shit side.

PUT MY LOVE
in a PICTURE

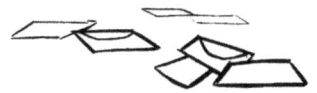

(A song about parental mistakes,
hoping the love is what is remembered.)

Meet me with softness. Meet me with rage.
Just say you'll meet me at end of day.

Take all of my mess-ups, my mixed-up words.
Give me a second chance, maybe a third.

Put my love in a picture when hurts leave you blind.
Put my love in a picture. Hearts mend with time.
Put my love in a picture. Remember me kind.
Put my love in a picture in a frame of mind.

I know you're leaving. That's how this goes.
Time stops for no one. Hearts open and close.
Take all my good wishes. All my best ways.
Sometimes we'll get it right, just not today.

Put my love in a picture when hurts leave you blind.
Put my love in a picture. Hearts mend with time.
Put my love in a picture. Remember me kind.
Put my love in a picture in a frame of mind.*

---

* Title track from *Put My Love In A Picture*, by Vashti Summervill, released 2022. Available on all streaming services and at www.vashtisummervill.com.

OVER-PARENTING REGRETS

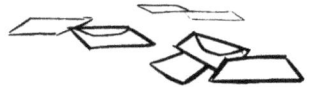

We all want to do better than our parents did.

Most of our parents want us to do better than they did.

I have played a part in teaching you the wrong things.

I forgive my parents for what I might have once called their failures or shortcomings. I hope you will reach this place with me one day.

I think I actually forgive myself for my failures and shortcomings.

No one sets out to do a bad job at parenting. We are all basically just trying to survive with the tools we have. Most of those tools came from how we were raised.

I often don't know how to deal with my own uncomfortable emotions. I don't know how to sit in uncertainty. I reach for my phone, Netflix, wine, or weed (just kidding, I was never into that) just as often as you do.

We are quick to be given pills instead of being taught to deal with uncomfortable emotions.

I have a very hard time watching you suffer, stumble, and traverse challenges. I wish I had learned how to handle myself in more productive ways when you were experiencing big feelings.

I know that in my discomfort with you being uncomfortable, I unintentionally fed your anxiety and depression. I unintentionally robbed you of opportunities to develop resilience, a strong self-identity, and a sense of capability.

This is probably my biggest regret.

Each time I slipped into problem solver or cheerleader mode I was well-intentioned, but now I know this did not help you.

I wish I had listened more. Helped you look at struggles and big feelings differently. I wish I had taught you to look at big feelings as teachers and as a necessary crucible for shaping a resilient, independent, capable, and compassionate human. You certainly are all these things but I could have helped make the path a little less brutal.

That's the irony. I thought I was saving you from pain when I was really just prolonging it. The suffering comes. The hurts come. I kept trying to shelter you from the inevitable instead of showing you how to navigate it. Maybe I contributed to keeping you stuck for longer than you needed to be.

I wish I had taught you to look at emotions and challenges as storms that pass through. We experience the storm and come out the other side. Another storm will come, but with each one we realize more profoundly that it is just a temporary visitor.

I think by being so scared of the storms, I trapped them, collected them. That is a lot of bottled-up thunder and lightning and energy begging for somewhere to go. We became storm collectors together.

If we had learned to just sit in it together, knowing it would pass, maybe so much wouldn't be stuck. Now we practice letting the storms pass, dancing with them, learning from them. With each passing storm, we get a little wiser and a little stronger.

There will always be storms. When we greet them with fear and resistance, they become hurricanes.

I wish I had taught you not to resist the storms. I wish someone had taught me this at a much younger age.

I'm going to call all of this what it is. I am an over-parenter.

Yes. This is my biggest parenting regret.

PLUGGED-IN
to the
WRONG THINGS

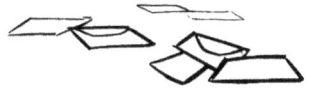

You tell me that you are not hopeful for your future. You think the world is ending. Sometimes I think it is ending too, but I can't stay in that place.

Your world, my world, seems to be based on competition and "likes."

We are constantly connected to information. We are drowning in noise and too much access and immediacy.

Instant gratification.

Instant devastation.

Repeated devastation. Gone are the days of boring news check-ins once or twice per day at most. I didn't want to watch Dan Rather or read a newspaper when I was a kid. Ew!

Now the news is force-fed to us all day every day. It seems we are being rewired to check it compulsively. When we try to disconnect, our brains can't stand more than a few minutes without wanting to seek information. But our hearts can't take much more. We aren't wired for this.

What is magnified by those with the megaphones isn't the whole story. I know that stories of ingenuity, magnificence, love, and compassion happen daily. But those don't seem to cut through the noise, so our perception gets pretty skewed toward the drama of doom and gloom.

We are a fiercely individualistic and "selfie" culture (I point the finger at myself too). And this seems like such a confusing paradox because the reality is most of us don't like ourselves much and sure don't treat ourselves with much kindness.

When we can't like and accept ourselves, how can we possibly like and accept others?

We can only treat others as nicely as we treat ourselves. A gentler world starts with the voice in our own heads. I wish I had modeled this a little differently for you. On occasion, I remember saying "Be your own best friend." I think we even set that as a New Year's resolution once. "I vow to treat myself as I would a dear friend."

What we plug into every day through our devices doesn't teach us to like and accept ourselves. We are taught that we need to buy, buy, and buy more. We must spend money in order to get a better body, better lashes, better things. It is an endless cycle of dissatisfaction. We are being programmed with a thirst that is unquenchable.

The earth is struggling. She feels really ill, but we just keep going. You don't understand why we keep going as we do. I don't understand it either.

I know that you are struggling to see a future for yourself. Then comes a pandemic.

And people are behaving badly. Really, really badly.

Seriously, what is happening? What are we supposed to do?

The problems seem too vast. Impossible to solve.

I think I have been checking the wrong news sources. I know there are people who have not lost hope. Once again, I know there are innovators actually coming up with solutions. They are lost in the noise.

Maybe it's time to unplug from this technological web and plug back into the web of life. Plug back into ourselves and people and the miracle of the earth and the mystery of all that is alive.

ABOVE AVERAGE

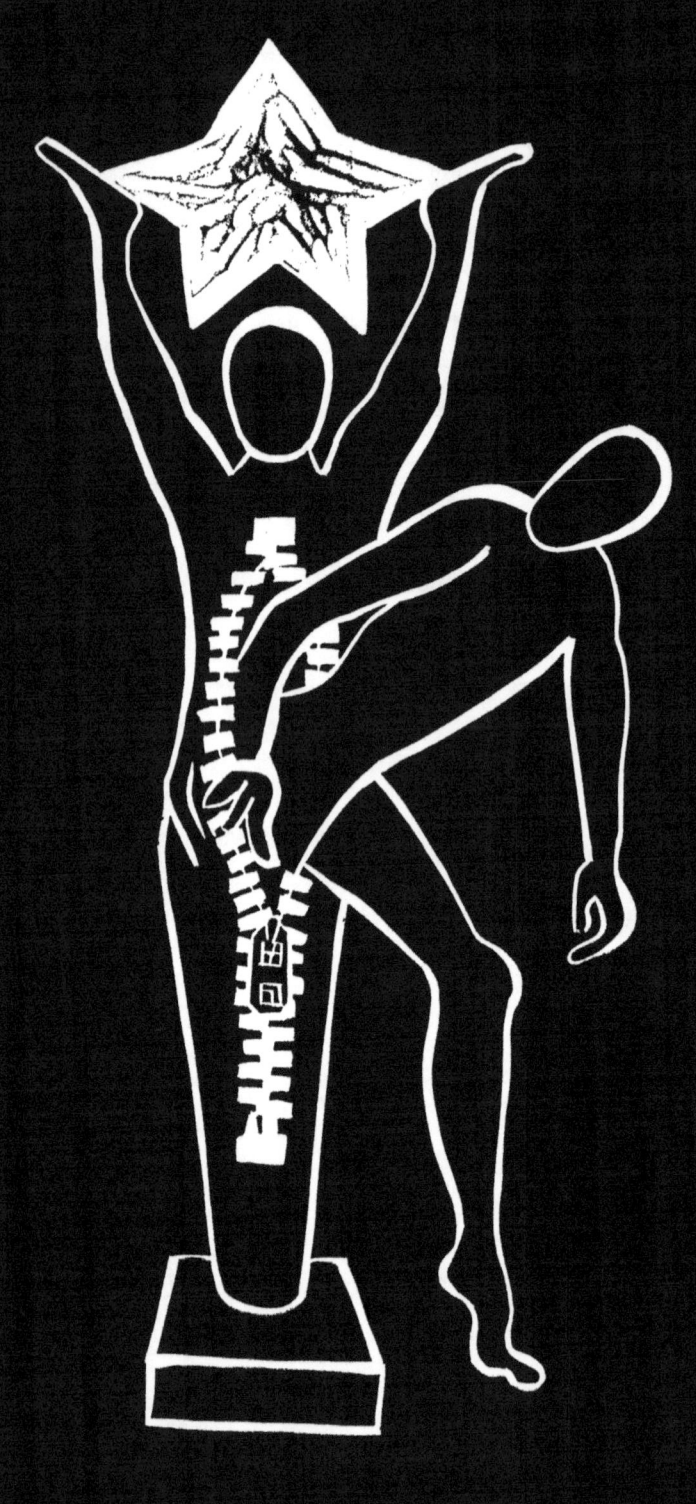

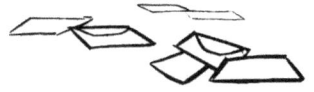

If you are average, you are nothing.

4.0 GPA = Meh. 4.8 is possible.

Don't you get it? The decisions you are making (or your parents are making for you) from the second you are born are either opening or slamming doors for you.

If you fall down, pull yourself up. Hide that you fell down in the first place. Don't be vulnerable. Don't show weakness (especially if you are male). Don't be a loser.

If you haven't played soccer since age five don't even bother trying it for fun later in life.

Nothing is recreational. Compete or don't do it.

That C, that social media post, that SAT score—they have ruined your chances for a good life.

And what about "likes" and "followers?" You can never have enough.

WE HAVE BECOME EXPERTS AT CATASTROPHIZING.

You often don't feel good enough. As parents, we operate from panic, trying to execute the perfect flight plan, to ensure that the best of the best is available to you. This puts a lot of pressure on you. We don't want to be this way but we are caught on the treadmill with everyone else.

A lot of that comes from our ego. What do we say to the other parents with the soccer star, the Ivy League applicant? We try not to feel like losers, but it's hard not to judge ourselves if what feels like a win is nothing more than, "My kid wants to live today."

I'm done with parental shame, judgment, and comparison.

If we are average in some areas, is that really a bad thing? There is so much more to a complete person.

"My kid gets C's but they aren't wrecked with anxiety."

"My kid doesn't play soccer but he takes walks and appreciates trees and sunsets."

"My kid doesn't want to be in college right now but she is thinking deeply about the world and how she wants to contribute. She is taking her time and I am ok with that."

I think we are looking at all of this wrong. I'm pretty sure we are focusing on and rewarding the wrong things.

I watch how you treat the checker at the grocery store, the person experiencing homelessness, and your grandparents. It is beautiful to watch.

You have struggled with your self-worth and the habit of comparing yourself to others. You are still trying to figure out who you are and how you work in the world.

You are still trying to figure out how to find joy in a world where you feel the injustices deeply.

You are still trying to figure out where you want to make your contribution.

It's ok, sweet girl. Take your time.

Get the C. Who cares. C doesn't mean failure or slamming doors. That C taught you something about yourself, right? It taught you something about your likes or dislikes. It taught you something about perseverance or working with someone you don't really click with. It probably taught you more than the content of the class itself. The learning that happens in the cracks is often more valuable than direct instruction. Remember that.

Try on all sorts of different jobs in your mind and in person. You can say you want to be a surgeon one day and an esthetician the next. Try it all on.

Change jobs. Change majors. This time in life is as much about figuring out who you are not as it is about figuring out who you are.

Remember your box of dress-up clothes? It's a lot like that. Give yourself permission to try on all sorts of things again and again and again. Don't forget that learning about yourself and the world is always happening. Value that learning.

Always give yourself permission to pivot. Just because you make one choice, it doesn't mean it has to be forever. Give yourself permission to shake things up when you feel called to try something else.

Just make sure that you are running toward something and not just running away from something.

When you feel average by the yardstick that society is measuring you by, just own it. Embrace it. Feel proud that you are blazing a trail that is unique to you, not just jumping on the one that everyone else thinks you should be on. This is how the world changes for the better—with innovators like you. Not just through people who strive for the 4.8 or the sports trophy. Those are great things if someone really wants them, but there seems to be a lot of pressure to measure everyone by those limited standards.

You are gifted with things that are unmeasurable and that society doesn't reward. I wish I had seen that earlier and focused on that. Some things just can't be measured.

Remember all the beautiful gifts that come so naturally to you. Your ability to find that lonely person and offer them connection. Your ability to accept people for who they are.

Keep being lovely and authentic with the checker at the grocery store, the person experiencing homelessness, and your grandparents. It is beautiful to watch and it is anything but average. You will find your way in your own time, my love.

DELAYED GRATIFICATION
GRATIFICATION
and GRIT

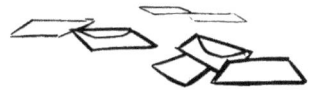

What a world you have grown up in! What a world we live in now!

Everything we want is at the tip of our fingers. Pizza? Boom! A movie? Choose from thousands, sit back and start streaming. Want a new pair of shoes or sheets? You can have it on your doorstep tomorrow—maybe even today!

Unfortunately, some of the things we truly need and deep down really want cannot be acquired in this way. Here are some things that don't happen that fast:

Learning an instrument.

Becoming an excellent athlete.

Writing a book.

Creating a beautiful work of art.

Becoming a master at anything.

Building a career.

Learning to manage your mind, your anxiety, and your low days.

Developing and maintaining deep and long-term relationships.

Your phone can't deliver any of that to you.

You have to work hard. You have to stumble and struggle and honestly, it isn't a bad thing. In the space of struggle is where most of the good stuff lies. Most of the best learning and the biggest "ahas!" in life lie smack dab in the middle of the messy struggle.

I'm actually at a place now where I welcome some struggle. I am proud of my grit and like to exercise it.

In my illusion that I should or could prevent you from suffering, I forgot that struggles and stumbles have been some of the best gifts in my life. I robbed you of some of yours. This was pretty bad thievery now that I reflect on it.

I have been trying to course correct and allow you to have your own stumbles and struggles. It's not easy for me, and I think this about-face may be confusing for you.

You have grit. I know you can do hard things. I know you can see instant gratification for what it is—a sham—and that the important things take time and hard work.

I wish for you the right amount of struggle.

I wish for you buckets of grit.

I wish for you piles of patience and self-compassion.

I wish for you the ability to reframe struggle as a beautiful thing.

I wish for you the satisfaction that comes from the lifelong pursuit of mastering something.

Mostly, I wish for you the ability to cultivate, maintain, and continually deepen all the relationships that are important to you. This includes your relationship with yourself.

May you be surrounded by people who value you, who are willing to persevere through the struggles and get even grittier with you.

I believe in you and your grit.

WHAT DOES *this* MOMENT REQUIRE?

I don't have to have everything figured out all at once. Neither do you.

Let's face it. Nothing will ever get wrapped up into a tidy box with a bow on top.

There is no perfect. There is no way to be a perfect parent, a perfect kid, or a perfect person.

Sometimes I find myself stuck in the past, in regret.

Usually, I find myself stuck in the future, planning, desiring things to be different...catastrophizing.

I forget to be right here, right now.

Right here and right now can feel messy and painful. But so do the past and the future. In the midst of all that is messy and painful, right here in the present, there is beauty and there are miracles.

You are a miracle. How do I ever forget that?

The fact that we are together in this life is a miracle. Why am I not celebrating that every single moment?

When I am forgetting everyday miracles, I am usually worried you are spending too much time on YouTube, Snapchat, TikTok, Gaming, or watching trash shows. I am worried you are wasting the precious commodity of time. I am worried that I can't seem to enforce boundaries around this.

I am worried about your study habits.

I am worried about your isolation and withdrawal.

I am worried about what a mess your room is.

I am worried about your social life.

I am worried about your depression.

I am worried about your substance use.

I am worried that you don't have enough coping skills.

I am worried that you don't like me or won't remember the good parts of me or your childhood.

I am worried about you.

I am caught in the mess and worry, so much of which comes from stories I am just telling myself. Stories that are getting bigger than they need to be. As the stories grow, so does the worry, and I am caught in a cycle.

I stop and once again consider the miracle.

I see the mess but I finally accept that the mess will always be there. That is being human.

I ask myself "What does this moment require of me?"

The moment might be asking me to say or do nothing.

The moment might be asking me to sit with my own discomfort.

The moment might be asking me to sit with you, but the moment might also be asking me to give you some space.

The moment might be asking me to lighten up and not take everything so seriously.

The moment might be asking me to take care of myself.

The moment might be asking me to simply find a way to connect with you human to human—not in our roles as parent and child.

Maybe you were on your screen for eight hours and I was on my screen for eight hours, and I yelled when I didn't want to, and you rolled your eyes and slammed a door. At the end of a day like this, if our hearts can genuinely connect, even for just a moment, we are winning.

So let's just take it moment-to-moment for a while. Let's ask, "What does this moment require?" and simply vow to do our best to pause and find the wisdom and kindness to give this moment what it needs.

You and me—we are going to be ok.

THE CRYING TREE

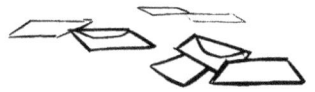

(A song I wrote about the feelings of helplessness
that come with having a child with depression.)

He sat under the crying tree on a ledge by the sea.
He makes a cut and the tree bleeds too.

He prayed under the crying tree, to be swallowed by the great green sea,
It would rise and the tree would bend.

The tree then whispers on the wind,
"I'll stay with you, that's all I can do. I'll stay with you to the other side."

He sat under the crying tree on that ledge, by the sea.
"I am here. But I don't know why."

He sat under the crying tree.
When thunder shook the ground, the tree shook too.
And the sky began to cry.

He spoke of monsters, madness, and unexplained sadness.
The unexplained sadness...

He asks again, "I am here but why?"

The tree then whispers on the wind,
"I'll stay with you, that's all I can do. I'll stay with you to the other side."

He sat under the crying tree watching the other boats sail in the great green sea, into the sun.

The warm, warm sun.

THOUGHTS *are* NOT FACTS

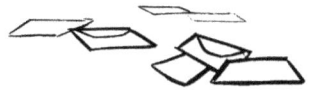

Thoughts are not facts. I long for you to learn this earlier than I did. TBH (you taught me that in text speak that means "to be honest"), I still struggle with this. But I have become aware that my thoughts can imprison me. At least this recognition gives me a choice. I can allow myself to stay with the thoughts—fertilize them, water them, and help them grow. Or, I can view them simply as clouds that will pass through.

The brain is wired to think. All that activity upstairs is basically a series of neurons firing somewhat randomly. Thoughts are random and as unpredictable as clouds. So when a thought breaks into my house, I can simply acknowledge it. "Hey there, thought. I see you but I'll also see you out." The more I practice this, the easier it gets. I hope that you can begin to practice this skill.

Contrary to the aphorism, practice does not make perfect. Practice makes progress. That's what I am doing—just trying my best to make a little progress in this area. And a little more the next day. Some days no progress or a little backsliding. Then back in the saddle and a little more improvement the next day. Perfection, which is only an illusion, can take a hike with unnecessary thoughts. I just wish for progress.

Escaping from inside a prison seems like a really tough thing to coordinate. Instead of living inside my thoughts, I am starting to drive past them, seeing them for what they are. And when I find myself, like some kind of crazy fool, trying to tunnel into that prison, I am learning to stop and back away. I don't need to figure anything out. I need to remember where I am, find activities that ground me—that get me out of my head. These activities are simple and easy. They feel good. I made you a list in case you ever need an idea to get yourself out of the mind trap:

- Sit in the sun with your eyes closed and imagine its warm, life-giving energy pouring gently into your body.

- Close your eyes and focus on sounds. Allow the sounds to come and go like thoughts but keep your focus on sounds. When your mind wanders, simply bring it back to the sounds.

- Take some deep breaths and simply notice where you feel your breath. Focus on that.

- Read a book.

- Drink some water.

- Get out in nature anytime you can.

Do anything but get on your phone or computer (note to self here).

RIVER *of* DISCOMFORT

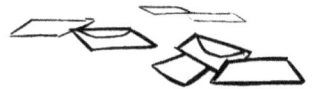

have come to believe that most of what we want in this life sits on the other side of a river of discomfort.

I think this goes for both of us.

For me, it's hard to see you experience emptiness, pain, and struggle. Letting you have your own experience is one of the rivers of discomfort that I must cross. It is a necessary separation of myself from you.

Just like me, you have to journey alone through the emptiness, pain, and struggle you feel—that's your river to cross. By alone, I mean that I cannot cross it for you. I can hug you, listen, and validate your feelings. I can hold you carefully in my heart as you make your way through, and I can be on the other side to celebrate with you, but I cannot do the paddling for you.

There have been times I have done the paddling for you and thought I had carried you safely to the other side. But a tributary of the same river was waiting for us, as if to say, "That's not how this works. You must cross on your own power and then I will flow on and so will you."

Every time you are stuck or I am stuck—not wanting to cross our own river—it is hard. But at the same time, it's familiar. It's the kind of hard we know about already, so it feels safer and more comfortable than the unknown currents of the river. Swimming in those currents is hard too, but at least we are moving forward. At least it is a productive hard. Being stuck is just hard and nothing good is happening. Stuck is like a seed trapped in a jar without the soil, water, and sunlight needed to grow.

I hope you will remember this and remind me when I need reminding. We can be brave. We can each cross our rivers of discomfort as they appear in our path. We can step into the currents of the unknown and be cleansed, refreshed, polished, and transformed in ways that only the river of discomfort can provide. Let's be brave together.

THE RIGHT KIND
of BUBBLE WRAP

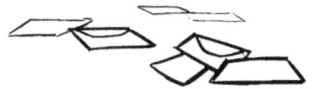

I have come to understand that parenting is a cycle of holding close and letting go—learning to let go, then pulling you close again, then letting you go again. With each letting go, you take another flight and your wings get stronger.

The trick is to know when to let go and to be very careful not to smother you when I pull you close.

When you left to backpack through Thailand, I was full of mixed emotions. I cycled from panic to peace, from fear to relief, then back to a head full of imagining worst-case scenarios, then back to peace again.

Mostly peace though. Peace because I knew it would be good for you. I wish I'd had the courage to do the same thing at that age. Your trip was a big letting go for me.

I knew you needed that time away to continue to grow and develop— away from family expectations. You needed the time and space to get to know yourself and the larger world and how you fit into it.

You needed the time to meet people and go on adventures, to allow one thing to lead to another as you experimented and learned through the twists and turns of your journey.

Talk about twists and turns. Who knew your six month trip would end in nine weeks due to a global pandemic? I was amazed by your grace and flexibility as you had to make an abrupt exit.

Way to pivot!

Now you are off on other adventures, each one an opportunity for you to experience new ways of being to see what fits you.

I have always told you there are many ways to make a good life.

Parenting and worry go hand in hand. As much as I know you need to spread your wings and fly and fall and fly again, it is very hard to let go. I found this quote in a book called, *The Language of Letting Go*, by Melody Beattie: "Letting go helps us to live in a more peaceful state of mind and helps restore our balance. It allows others to be responsible for themselves and for us to take our hands off situations that do not belong to us."

You took the reins on that trip. It was yours to make. It was yours to own.

I had to work hard to tame my anxiety because there was so much that was unknown. I had no way of knowing if you would be ok.

There are never any guarantees of safety. Not even in our own backyard.

With each letting go, I have to trust you and know that we have done our best work as parents. I have to practice finding that feeling of peace, knowing that you are learning and growing. I have to remind myself that you aren't five years old and that you are strong, wise, capable, and resilient.

Wherever you go you will make many new friends. I've seen you interact with people who work in Trader Joe's and strangers on the street. I don't need to worry about your ability to connect with people. You are quite good at that.

I also know that you will always meet angels along the way. Beautiful souls who will help you at the exact moment you need a hand.

As Mr. Roger's mother would say to him, "Look for the helpers. You will always find people who are helping."

I know your heart and know you will be a helper to many along their journey as well. Your empathy really is your superpower.

Sometimes your plans are loose—too loose for my taste. Your timeline is different than my timeline. But then I remind myself it's YOUR timeline—not MINE.

As much as I sometimes wish I could, I know I can't wrap you in rolls of bubble wrap and protect you from everything. I might smother you with my bubble wrap (texts, phone calls, worried communications) if I am not careful. Too much bubble wrap prevents you from spreading your wings. What bird can fly with a bunch of extra weight wrapped around its wings? That's what parental expectations and attempts to outguess and protect from everything are—extra weight on a kid.

I also know that too much bubble wrap robs you of important bruises. Bruises that help you learn resilience.

If I smother you in bubble wrap, I help create a story in your mind that you are incapable.

I'm going to choose to wrap you in a very different kind of bubble wrap. I am choosing to wrap you in my confidence in YOUR ability, in my belief in YOUR wisdom and skill. I want you to fly on all your adventures knowing you got this, even when you have some inevitable crashes.

I also wrap you in my faith and overall belief that people are good and that those people you need will appear on your journey when you need them.

I vow to continue to meditate on all of your strengths.

I vow to refrain from worried speculation, and instead to use my energy to visualize a journey filled with meeting wonderful people, an incredible widening of perspective, and adversity and challenges that you are prepared to take on.

I vow to look at adversity and challenge as necessary tools to strengthen you.

I visualize and anticipate unexpected surprises that will reveal your next adventure, the next path, the next chapter.…These are the things I have to visualize in order to keep my inner peace.

I will look forward to enjoying your excitement as you share tales from each adventure.

I vow to maintain calm and a clear head when you call and something has gone wrong.

I vow to not over-communicate or demand frequent communication from you.

I vow to let your journey be 100% your journey.

This is the kind of bubble wrap you need. This is the kind of bubble wrap that will best serve you.

Margaret Rutherford says, "Your child's life will be filled with fresh experiences. It's good if yours is as well."

I have lots of plans for my own adventures. Wish me luck too.

RELEASE

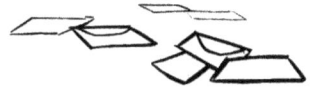

I commit to releasing small thinking.

I commit to myself to stop catastrophizing, to stop mentally practicing for worst-case scenarios.

I commit to doing my own work.

I celebrate the good that I have already done as a parent.

I celebrate the brilliance that already exists within you, which I had nothing to do with.

I celebrate the miracles and the beauty that are everywhere waiting for me to simply notice.

I release the illusion that I was somehow ultimately responsible for your journey. What I held onto, what I thought I controlled, never was mine. I just made both of us sick pretending I was in the driver's seat.

I gather the energies of goodness and light and I release your awakening to you.

I gather the energies of goodness and light as I continue my own awakening.

SETTLING
MY GLITTER

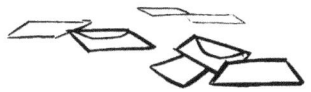

From time to time, every human being flips their switch. When it happens, it is involuntary. It is physiological. Some call this moving from our upstairs, more rational brain, to our downstairs, fight, flight, or freeze survival brain.

It is a feeling of boiling blood, a tightness in the throat and chest. It is the feeling of imminent explosion or implosion, depending on who you are.

I flipped my switch a lot with you.

My switch still flips. The only thing I can hope for is that when these events occur, I can take a step back and observe my internal experience as it unfolds without immediately reacting.

I remember times when one of us would flip our switch and then the other one would. Then it was a duel. Sometimes you would ask me to back down, to leave your bedroom and save the conversation for later. But I would dig in. I would insist that we work out whatever was happening right then and there. It never went well.

I'm trying to get better at timing conversations. You always seemed a bit wiser about that than me. Perhaps I thought that being a "good" parent meant immediate resolution.

I now know that no teaching, understanding, correcting, reconciliation, or connecting can happen with a flipped switch.

I read an article once about a therapist who used a glitter globe in therapy sessions with teens. She would shake it up until the bits of glitter chaotically floated in the once-clear water. She would explain to teens that this is what happens when your nervous system is upset. This is what it's like in your brain when your switch is flipped. She would then coach the teens to "settle their glitter" before taking action. Adults need coaching on this too.

I will continue to work on "settling my glitter" before responding to you. I will also give you space and time for your glitter to settle. I will stop trying to force communication. I also promise not to yell, "Settle your glitter!" in a snarky tone. Maybe you could give me the same courtesy.

And when the clear water returns, we might have a chance to learn and love more deeply.

A WAY *to*
VIEW MISTAKES

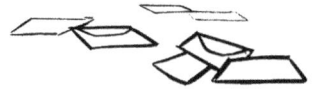

I want to be a person who views mistakes as a window to learning.

I don't want to look at people's mistakes as character flaws.

I don't ever want to stop believing in a person's capacity to grow and change.

I hope that people will extend this grace to me too. I hope that you will extend this grace to me.

I have tried to be gracious when you make mistakes.

I have tried to understand that sometimes it is just teen impulsivity.

I have tried to understand that sometimes your mistakes came out of a desperate need to find connection and to be liked.

Maybe you can consider viewing some of my mistakes as coming out of fear for your wellbeing and the short-temperedness that comes with being weighed down by adult responsibilities.

I hope you can understand that some of my mistakes are born out of a desperate need for self-preservation and to connect and be liked, too.

I really like the "three times" concept for mistakes. It goes something like this:

- The first time is a mistake.

- The second time is a choice.

- The third time is a pattern.

I can be very gracious with a mistake.

I can offer advice when there is a choice.

I can hold a boundary when there is a pattern.

I can work to do this without anger, letting the consequences do the teaching. That is my goal anyway. But sometimes I do get caught in the trap of taking things personally. This is also something I am working on.

What I am talking about here are the kind of mistakes that affect your health and well-being and the well-being of others.

It is my job to hold appropriate and life-preserving boundaries. These boundaries are connected to my end game as a parent, which is to raise a capable, compassionate, independent, and resilient human.

Someone taught me a valuable process for handling mistakes. I use it whenever I can. It is a process of self-reflection:

- Can you describe the mistake you made?

- Who might this mistake have harmed?

- What amends do you need to make?

- What will you do next time you are faced with a similar situation?

This process is a guide to help us solve our own problems, to learn and grow from our own mistakes, and to become the best version of ourselves.

Using this process, you can figure out for yourself what amends need to be made, without me lecturing you or punishing you.

I might have to step in sometimes with another perspective or offer some input, but you are the one with the power and responsibility to choose how you will handle your own mistakes.

It isn't so complicated. It's a natural part of life. When we can own our mistakes and repair our relationships, we can look each other in the eye, say "I love you," and move on.

THE REAL
BANK ACCOUNT

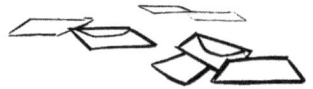

For some reason negative interactions are so much louder than positive ones. I'm sure you have been appreciative more often than I have noticed or received.

I recently read (yes—I learned this from one of those "dumb books" I keep reading—I don't intend to stop) that it takes five positive interactions to balance one negative interaction. All of these interactions make up our Relationship Bank Account.

We are human. We will behave in ways we wish we hadn't, so we would all be wise to make sure our Relationship Bank Account balance is well in the black (which means in the positive—"in the red" means we have a deficit).

I look at the Relationship Bank Account as an accumulation of goodwill. It's less about what we do than the way we make someone feel. It reminds me of a quote by Maya Angelou, "People will forget what you said and people will forget what you did but people will never forget how you made them feel."

I'm sure that my behaviors have often felt like a river of nagging corrections gushing toward you. I'm not trying to excuse this, but the reality is that sometimes parents are just trying to survive the busyness and responsibility of meeting everyone's needs, managing schedules, etc. No one taught me the concept of the Relationship Bank Account when I was younger.

Maybe that is part of the problem. We are all trying to cram in so much that we forget how we are making other people feel.

I need you to know that sometimes your words feel like a torrent of criticisms too. Sometimes I feel like you don't see my good efforts. I often feel like you just ignore me unless you want something. You might feel the same.

Maybe we could both try to make more deposits and take fewer withdrawals from our Relationship Bank Accounts.

I know I have made you feel small and incapable sometimes. I am aware of this and have been making efforts to hold my tongue. I believe that holding our tongue is a deposit.

I believe that making a repair when I am not being the person I mean to be is a deposit. So when you see me take a pause and say, "I am not being the person I mean to be right now," or, "I am not being the parent I mean to be right now," you can know that I am making an effort to course correct and be better.

I know I am not perfect. I want to show you I can own my mistakes. I am committed to being a lifelong learner and a lifelong self-improver. I have made an internal pact to continue to heal and grow myself and my relationships throughout my life.

I also believe that showing genuine interest in your world, in the things that interest you, in your profound thoughts—these are ways to make a deposit.

I am truly fascinated and delighted by the way your brain works, the way you see things, by your creativity, humor, and wit. You have a lot to teach me. Have I ever told you that you are my greatest teacher?

I will continue learning about the unique being you are.

I will try not to do it in an annoying, overly question-y way. I'm sure I will botch it and I'm sure I will still annoy you at times. That's part of the dance.

Perhaps it doesn't have to be all annoyance all the time. As I work to soften my heart toward you, maybe you could also soften your heart toward me.

I hope you will give me a chance.

I know this is the most important bank account balance there is.

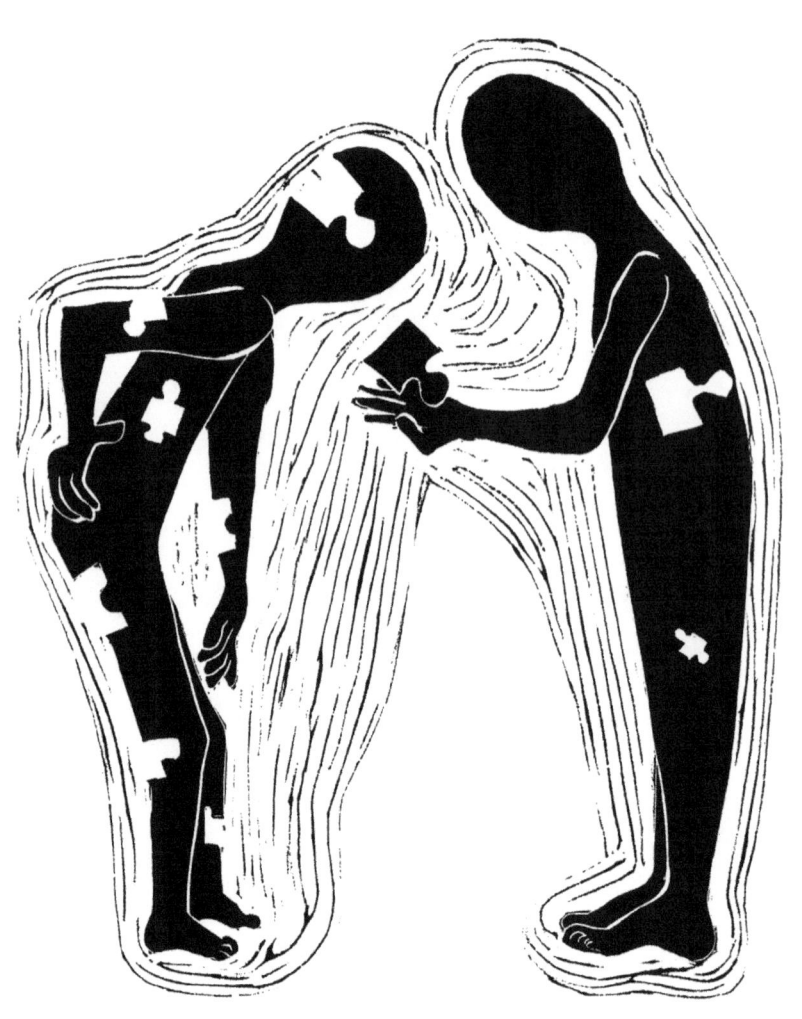

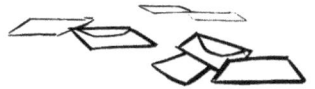

The other day we were stuck on a couple of issues. Again.

I reacted in a way that shut down productive communication. Again.

Walls went up between us. Again.

I ponder the many times we've been at this impasse. The heaviness that overtakes me in these moments feels like someone has placed bags of concrete on each of my shoulders. There's a tightness in my stomach and I feel a bone-deep exhaustion. "Again?"

We went our separate ways for a bit. We regrouped. We always do. We regroup but we don't really repair. We don't really learn about one another's heart.

And then it hit me…

Reactivity comes as a result of feeling threatened in some way.

What do some of those threats look like from my point of view? Often, I see a behavior or a choice you make and I begin to make assumptions. A negative story grows in my head and then deep mother fear enters. Fears for your safety. Fears for your future. Fears about my own failings as a parent.

That's when I react. It's an automatic impulse to prevent imagined catastrophe. The root is not anger or control just for control's sake. The root is usually the fear that feels like it might swallow me. Of course reactivity begets more reactivity, and I feel you slip away, which scares me more.

I also react when I feel my time being threatened, or my sense of order and control, when I am juggling too many things and my margins of extra time are paper thin to nonexistent. Perhaps it is my sense of self that feels threatened when I don't think I am seen by you as an actual person.

This reactivity cycle seems to go both ways. It's a lousy game of Follow the Leader. Sometimes I lead and you follow. Sometimes you lead and I follow.

Your reactivity must also be a result of you feeling threatened in some way. I have some guesses.

Maybe your sense of capability and independence is feeling threatened. Perhaps your privacy and autonomy feel at risk or perhaps you don't feel seen for who you really are and your sense of self feels fragile.

When things calm down a bit, I share this new way of thinking about reactivity. We have a conversation. An actual, productive conversation.

We soften and soften some more. We learn something about one another's hearts.

We both feel seen as people, not just as "mother" or "child."

We agree that focusing on one another's reactivity is what keeps us stuck. We also agree that we both need to work on our reactivity and find new ways to express what we are feeling. We acknowledge that when we just focus on the other's reactivity, we miss an important opportunity to see what is beneath it and learn something important about one another and perhaps ourselves.

We continue to soften and agree to exchange our old lens for this new one and see if it keeps us from getting stuck in old places. We discover a new piece of this puzzle of being human. We begin a new story. Together.

SHARED EXPERIENCES CHANGE MY BRAIN

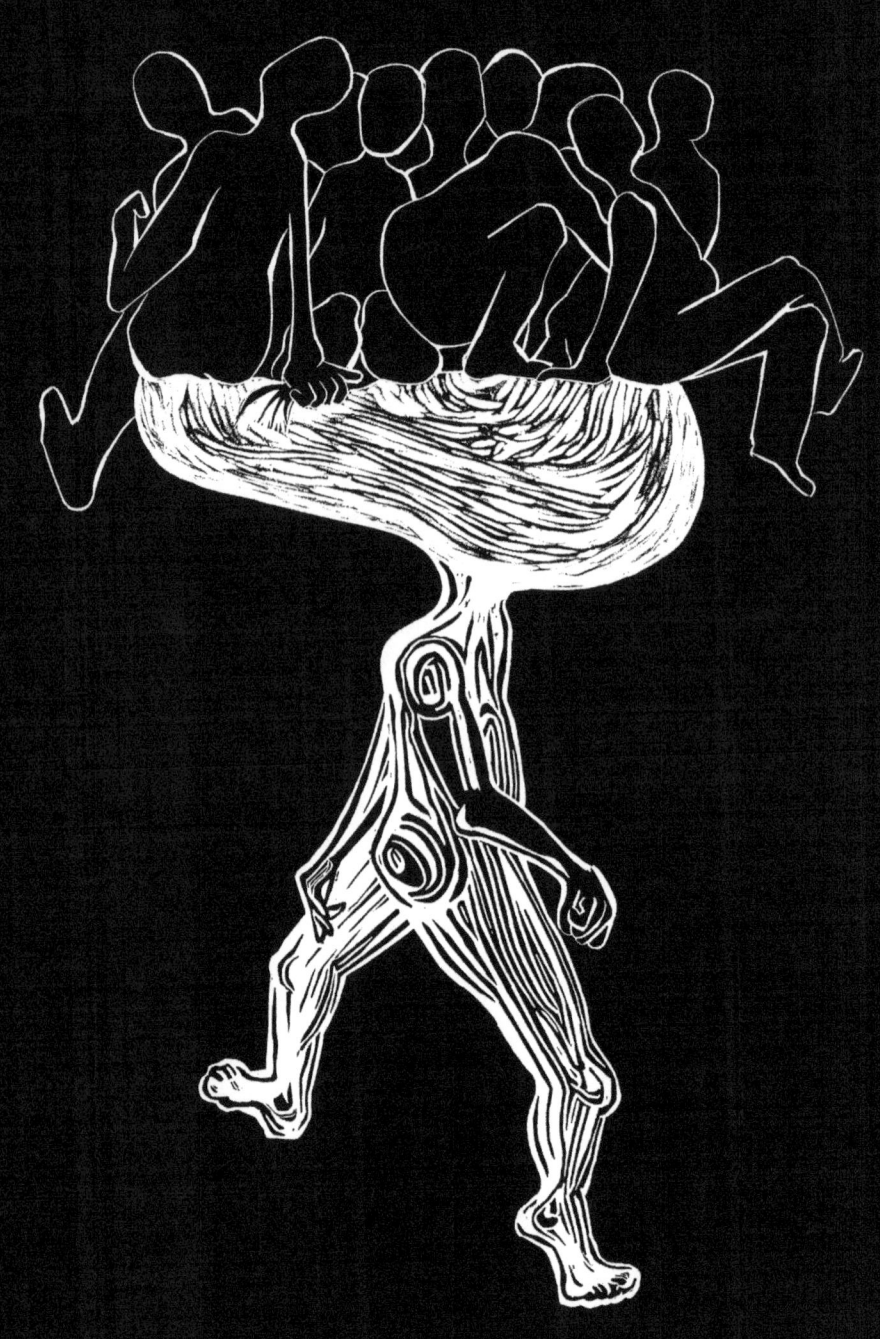

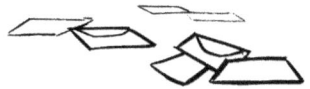

Your dad recently taught me a big lesson in a gentle and loving way. I know that you have been witness to us learning our way through an imperfect marriage. I know I have modeled love and grace and patience as well as judgment, impatience, and disdain. Hopefully, the scales of your memory will tip on the side of the former.

As you know, your dad and I have some shared interests. I have battled jealousy and feelings of inferiority when I felt compared to him or when successes came easier for him. This is a shadow side of me that I am not proud of. I am working to shine the light and shift.

Recently he was working on a creative project. I couldn't believe how much time he was spending at his computer trying to get it right. My narrative was that the family was not as high on the priority list as his own pursuits, and that he was escaping relationship with us by focusing on that instead. And yes…I was jealous that he was prioritizing his creativity. I wanted to prioritize my creativity as well, but felt I needed to do things for the family first. While there is some validity to my feelings that I carry some fairly heavy loads for the family, in my martyrdom I am sometimes blind to the loads Dad carries.

And the bigger truth is that I have had roadblocks of my own making that prevented me from pursuing the things I feel drawn to. Mostly it is fear that I'm not good enough. I would postpone taking action because of this fear, then tell myself I wasn't allowed to do my project because I had to do all these other things for the family instead.

Who was going to do it if not me? That kind of thinking squashed any kind of creative problem solving.

I recently got brave and launched my own creative project very similar to Dad's. It has come with a big serving of Humble Pie. I had no idea how hard it was to do what he was doing until I tried. The learning curve has been steep. It had to become a priority and I'm sure Dad has felt like he has seen me less.

I have tried to make amends with him for my previous attitude. "I'm sorry I was so hard on you. This is difficult." You know what? He didn't gloat. He wasn't filled with schadenfreude (look it up—might help you win a trivia night). He was graceful and gentle. When I asked him why he wasn't gloating because, frankly, I was awful, he just said, "We are closer to understanding one another. We now have a shared experience."

I want to remember this and treat those I love with more grace and less assumption, and fewer all-about-me thoughts. I'm going to work on this in my relationship with you too. Thanks for being patient with me as I imperfectly muddle through it all.

POWER IN *the* DELICIOUS PAUSE

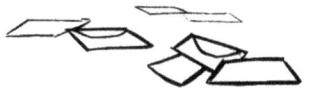

P ausing is actually a parenting superpower. It is easier said than done.

It is much easier to spin off in habitual and reactive ways. Lucky us, our brains can be rewired, but it takes a lot of intentional effort.

It takes slowing down.

It means taking a breath as a pathway out of my head, into my body, and into the space of a powerful, pretty little pause.

I know tremendous power exists between stimulus and response.

I know I don't need to say everything that I think I do.

After some of our more difficult times, my mantra became, "Is what I want to say meant to correct, control, or connect?"

I know that I should opt for connection a thousand times over control and correction.

Sometimes that connection is made by me keeping my mouth shut.

I know this but it is so hard. I am working on it.

Pause.

Pause.

Inhale.

Exhale.

Inhale, 2, 3.

Exhale, 2, 3, 4, 5, 6.

Inhale, 2, 3, 4.

Exhale, 2, 3, 4, 5, 6, 7, 8.

Repeat. Repeat. Repeat.

Ah…delicious, nourishing pause and breath. There you are. You never fail me.

DISSONANCE

Your generation is asking some really important questions. Watching the generations before you working obsessively, consuming voraciously, and always in pursuit of more. You are questioning the so-called "American Dream."

While we have had the gift of material abundance, you can see the toll it takes to maintain it all.

You seem to want to be less weighed down. I see you searching for purpose and meaning beyond the pursuit of material goods. You long for experiences over possessions.

I think that in your heart you want simplicity. You want to define what enough is and stop the chase for more.

If you figure this out, please teach me.

However, I do notice some dissonance here.

It has to do with the place you spend so much of your time. Social media seems to give you a different message than the one your internal compass is giving you. Buy this. Do this to your body. Live here. Be a Kardashian. If you don't get the "likes" and the followers, well—You. Are. Nothing.

On some level, I know you can see through this, but you are having trouble visualizing and creating the life you want—a new dream in the system that exists. You continue to make efforts to like and accept yourself just as you are.

This quote by Caroline Caldwell seems spot on. "In a society that profits from your self-doubt, liking yourself is a rebellious act."

Maybe we can be rebels together? Maybe you can teach me.

This dissonance is part of what is making you sick.

This dissonance, the questioning, and the invitation to explore new ways of living also give me hope for a better future for all of us.

STOPPING *the* CHASE: ONE MORE THING SYNDROME

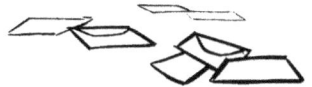

How much is enough? We are told at every turn that we don't have enough. That we aren't enough.

That self-doubt keeps us consuming. That is what "they" want us to do. You have become more aware of how capitalism works than I am. You want to rebel against the system that hurts the planet and a huge percentage of the people trying to live on it.

But you aren't immune to it. You don't want to conform but I see you struggle to like yourself from the outside in instead of from the inside out. I am not immune. I am the same.

Just so you know, I have never been better than you. I have never known more than you. I had to put on my parenting hat and pretend, but I'm basically just as lost as you are, hanging on by my fingernails. I'm pretty much winging everything.

I remember giving you a silver ring in the shape of a bow. I gave it to you when I could see your sense of self was more fragmented than it should be—even for a junior high girl. I wanted you to know that you are a gift to the world. That you are enough. You left it on a counter in the school bathroom and someone took it. Maybe that girl needed to know that she is enough too.

In this quest to be enough, we are taught to chase material wealth, prestige, and status. It's One More Thing Syndrome. If I can just get into THAT college, I will be enough. If I can get THAT house or THAT car, I will be enough. If I can get my abs or my legs or my butt to look like THAT, I will be enough. But nothing will ever be enough. There is always one more thing. When the truth is: THIS is enough. THIS body and THIS spirit we have each been given is enough.

What I didn't tell you was that I, too, have One More Thing Syndrome. I will be happy when I get X, when Y happens, or when I look like Z. I modeled this.

I modeled chasing excess. The nicer house. The nicer things for the nicer house. The nicer car, clothes, phones, etc.

Excess and One More Thing syndrome have caused disease of the body and the mind. Overconsumption and constantly chasing everything does not lead to wellness.

My chase for more is coupled with my lack of awareness of and gratitude for what I have.

I have been studying some of the great teachers of mindfulness. Thich Nhat Hanh says that a grain of rice contains the whole world—the earth, the rain, the clouds, the farmer, the people who brought it from farm to table, and the hands that prepared it. When I look at a grain of rice in this way, it makes me aware that when I have one grain of rice, I have a lot. When I have an entire bowl of rice, I have a LOT of a lot.

When we look at all that goes into bringing us the world of things, we might define enough differently and only consume what we need to nourish our bodies and minds. The planet might heal if more of us lived like this. Kids might not have to live with all this anxiety and uncertainty about their future. If each of us can figure out how to live with enough, more people might have enough.

We might finally find ease and peace on our life's journey.

I am enough. You are enough. Isn't the whole world contained in us, just like that grain of rice?

I wish for you just enough.

I CAN'T TAKE ANY MORE ARROWS

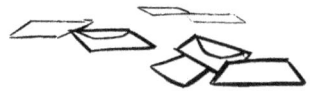

'm not trying to be toxic. Please stop saying things like this.

I can't take any more arrows.

I'm trying to understand your world. I really am.

I'm trying to survive.

You tell me you are nothing like me. It is human nature to not want to be like your parents.

But words like this do hurt. A parent is still a human. I think you forget this sometimes.

I can't take any more arrows.

Every time you are out at night, I don't want to assume the worst of you.

I don't want to be suspicious all the time. I'm just really scared of the world you are growing up in.

I will admit that sometimes I am so caught up in our roles as parent and child that I forget you are an autonomous human being. I am trying to see you.

You tell me that I don't understand depression. You say things like, "That's not how anxiety works." You have never asked if I experience anxiety.

I am trying to understand your world. I really am.

I think you minimize your substance use. You think I exaggerate it. You don't like me questioning it. You like to remind me that I don't understand how weed works and you act like it is harmless and actually a healthy supplement.

By the by—do you kids all share a script? Many of my friends report hearing the same things from their kids.

You remind me of every botched response I have ever had. Like the time I ruined your Halloween Party because we thought there was weed in our house. I do know I would handle it differently if I could have a do-over. I was scared. There is no playbook for navigating these situations.

But I can't take any more arrows.

You tell me that I don't do enough to be an anti-racist or for police reform or climate change. You are right. I'm not trying to ignore all that is wrong with the world. Just because I'm not at your level of rage doesn't mean I am not sad about injustice and, in my own way, working for justice. But I need you to know that your anger doesn't seem productive. Yes...I could do more, but I also have loads of adult responsibilities. I'm trying to survive the world and parenting all at once.

Please try to get to know me a little better. Please make some efforts to understand my heart and mind—what I align with and what I would like to see change in this world. I will do the same for you. You have taught me a lot already and for this I thank you.

I can't take any more arrows.

I am often at a loss and don't know what to do. This is the reality.

One thing I know to be true is that I keep showing up. Mistakes and all. I roll up my sleeves, keep trying to learn and do better. I will make mistakes. But I will continue to make repairs and do my best to be a better person than I was the day before.

I am lost too.

I am scared.

I am exhausted.

I am drowning in the noise of the world and the wilderness of parenting and worrying about the well-being of others.

I can't take any more of your arrows. But I will.

I know that you are just trying to develop your identity and figure out how to navigate this world. It isn't personal.

Let me repeat that. My highest self does know that this isn't personal.

BEHAVIOR is ALWAYS a MESSAGE

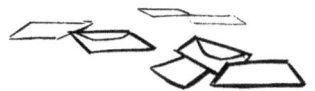

The eye-rolling, the yelling, the withdrawing, the isolating, the lying. The general grumpiness. The substance use. Pretending not to care. The screen addiction. The lack of motivation and follow-through. The school resistance. The risk-taking. The self-harm.

None of this is a personal affront against me. I often take it personally. But now I can see that it isn't about me.

The behaviors, while annoying and often hard to take, are not personal. Behavior is always a message. I don't always know what that message is, and I'm not sure you do either. I can make some guesses.

You are seeking connection, belonging, hope, security, and a sense of purpose.

You need to know that your thoughts matter. You need to like yourself. You need to feel valued. You need to feel understood.

As I row my boat through times when your behaviors feel not just annoying but downright hurtful, I'm going to try to lead with more curiosity, empathy, and love (always love).

Perhaps you have never felt understood by me. Maybe you feel that I can't see you as a complete person but just as my child—as some "thing" to be managed and molded in a way that aligns with my own conditioning, belief system, and internal experience. I fear there is some truth in this.

Announcement: I release you to become exactly who you want to be.

Perhaps you feel trapped in a world that expects you to conform in ways you feel in your bones are not right or healthy. When I widen my perspective and look at behaviors differently, I see you differently. I see the courage you have to question the world in ways that I definitely did not at your age. Instead of taking it personally, I will join you and gently blow on the embers of your courage in hopes that it grows into a productive fire, readying you and the world for new ways of being human. When I can look past the behavior and slow down and really listen to you, I am grateful for the ways you continually teach me.

Perhaps you feel insecure, vulnerable, alone. Maybe you are trying to learn to like and connect with yourself. I'm pretty sure you are looking for deep connection with others and trying to find your tribe and the journey seems very lonely at times.

I wonder if your behavior is your way of saying you need hope and the lack of hope is paralyzing you. I know that some days it is hard to get out of bed. It is hard to know where to start. It is hard to take care of yourself in the most basic ways.

Perhaps you feel like you will never have enough money and wonder how you will ever be fully independent and able to take care of yourself. You don't like asking for help from your parents but feel really stuck.

I wonder if you often feel angry about parts of your childhood. There might be some resentment over not feeling seen or understood. Perhaps you feel hurt by the times I was angry, the excessive lectures and the punishments.

Often, I did not give you the space you needed to BE and to BECOME.

I'm sure you feel hurt about confidences not kept by me. In my attempt to process and survive the ride, I talked behind your back. My fear, anxiety, skill deficits, need for acceptance, and need to feel confident, all led to me oversharing. I ran to other people instead of turning inward and modeling for you how to sit with fear, anxiety, and vulnerability. I ran to other people instead of tapping into my own strength and wisdom. I ran away from myself seeking comfort and approval from others.

I was not calm. I was reactive. Those behaviors weren't actually about you. They were messages coming from my insecurities as a parent. They were unhealthy, panicky expressions of my deep fears about what was going on with you. Now I am learning better tools to work through my fears and challenging emotions. I was simply doing my best to survive the ride at that time.

Perhaps you feel stuck in your own head, looping the same paths you have traveled for a long time. These paths are filled with hecklers telling you that your body doesn't look right, that your brain is broken, that you will never be enough or have enough, that the world is ending, and that you are sick.

Sometimes you find relief by self-medicating with substances. You know this isn't the best thing for you but it is a complex cycle to break.

I wonder if you feel anger towards me for modeling alcohol as a normal part of everyday life. I think that I believed I was always under control and modeling moderate use. While I wasn't drunk and "off-the-rails partying," I had wine way too often. I was also using it as an escape to numb out and survive life's stressors. I am sorry I modeled that. Once again, my behavior was a message too. I am grateful I am learning to listen and respond to these messages in healthier ways.

I think you see lots of possibilities in the world and so much that you want to experience. However, it might seem overwhelming to figure out how to get from here to there.

I am trying to see you. I am trying to look past the behaviors, to not take them personally, and working to discover what need you are trying to get met. Once we understand this about ourselves and others, we can more wisely choose how we respond. I'm really working on this in my personal journey.

May we both learn how to navigate the normal suffering of life in healthy ways. May we both be free from unnecessary suffering, much of which is created in our own minds and is born from our reactions. May we both be well. May we both be creative problem solvers and emotional detectives. May we both rid ourselves of the habit of taking everything so personally. May we both trust ourselves and our inner knowing. May we find abundance in that which is just enough—no more, no less. May we know security. May we be well. May we find joy. May we know peace. May we be authentic. May you be YOU and me be ME.

FIELDING ENERGY

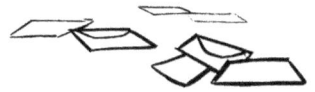

(This letter is written from the perspective of a parent of daughters. We acknowledge that there are many sexuality challenges and traumas across the gender spectrum that are not addressed here.)

You think I am a victim-blamer when I bring up the need for personal responsibility for how you dress and what you are smoking or drinking.

Consent is consent. No means no. I believe this from the bottom of my heart.

There is no justification anyone can make for non-consensual sex—that is assault.

You should be able to dress any way you want. But I worry. I am scared. I wonder if you can field the energy you will attract, especially if you have been smoking weed or drinking. We have a generation of boys who have seen young women portrayed in hyper-sexualized ways and have had access to porn that does not portray normal relationships. I know that girls access it too. It's a mess and makes my head spin.

Not that many in my generation had a lot of training in healthy relationships and sexuality either. My education is sort of like what you describe you got in school. "Don't have sex before marriage; you will get pregnant or die!"

But my generation wasn't bombarded with the same amount of imagery and videos, and didn't have access to what basically amounts to a really graphic "adult" store at the tip of our fingers 24 hours per day.

Dad, having experience being a teenage boy, said that he doesn't know if he would have had the self-control at age fourteen to avoid the temptation of that kind of access. He and his friends anxiously awaited the Sears catalog (yes—that was once a store) so they could flip through the bra ads. One friend's dad had a Playboy magazine or two tucked away—they would sneak in so they could look through it. The access was nothing like it is today.

I am scared about the effects of a mental diet of gratuitous programming that is so easy to consume and over-consume for both males and females.

I am not a victim blamer. I want you to be able to dress how you want and attend parties, but you have to take into account the way the world is and hedge your bets in a way that keeps you safe.

You say "Why is it on us? What about the males?" I have no response. There is just so much pornography, dysfunction, distorted thinking, noise, substance abuse, and mental and emotional anguish…this is what is. You have to protect yourself.

I WONDER ABOUT *a* DAY *in* YOUR LIFE

I find myself wondering what a day in your life is like. Do you ever wonder that about me?

What does it feel like waking up as you? What do you look forward to in your day? What do you dread?

I wonder what it is like for you walking in the halls of your school. Are you comfortable in your you-ness? Do you have friends to hang out with between classes? Do you worry about the looks you are getting in the hall? I wonder if lunchtime is a fun time with your friends or if you worry about having people to eat with? Do you think people are judging you all the time?

I wonder what it is like for you to feel you need to keep up your online persona while I simultaneously yell "For the love of God, get off your phone!"

I wonder if you feel like most adults like you. Do you feel like your teachers like you?

I wonder how I have made you feel with all my parenty-ness. Do you feel like I like you?

I wonder what you think about your future prospects. I wonder if you are able to find small moments of joy throughout your day or if it is all tasks and anxiousness. I hope it's the former. I wonder what small things in life you are able to savor.

I wonder what it feels like to be a young person and see so much division in this world. I wonder what it feels like to be a young person and worry about climate change. I bet the worry feels different than it does for older people. Believe me, I worry. But I wonder what this kind of worry would have done to me at your age.

In spite of some of the divisions in our world, I wonder what it feels like to grow up in a time when there is so much more acceptance of differences. Some of the tough stuff of this world sure seems to have catalyzed a generation of open-minded and accepting humans. Is this how you see yourself and the majority of your peers?

I wonder what it is like for you when you lie down at night and try to close your eyes and go to sleep. What thoughts make you smile and what thoughts keep you up?

I wonder what it is like to be in your skin. Do you like yourself? I wonder if sometimes you speak to yourself in cruel ways. Or are you sometimes able to look at yourself in the mirror in gentle ways and say, "You are doing just fine in life and I love you!"

PLANTING SEEDS, LOVING MYSELF, BEARING WITNESS

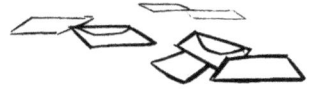

Sometimes my self-talk becomes negative and I judge myself for all the parenting woulda-coulda-shouldas.

But then I remember to find a little self-compassion.

I remember that, even though I often messed up or couldn't find the right words, I also modeled some positive things.

I know you witnessed me being compassionate and kind most of the time.

I know you witnessed me being honest.

I know you witnessed me showing up and trying again and again in many areas of my life.

I know you witnessed grit and perseverance through challenges.

I know you witnessed me making amends.

I know you witnessed me course correcting when needed.

These are the things most parents want their kids to embody. More learning happens because of who we are than what we say. It certainly doesn't happen through lecturing, nagging, or preaching.

I remind myself that everything you observed was planting seeds.

I remind myself that these seeds will germinate, sprout, grow and produce for years to come.

Not that I have been your only teacher. I certainly don't take credit for who you are and who you are becoming. I am grateful that I have been able to play a small part.

I thank myself for the things I have done right.

I am proud of the ways I model creativity, grit, perseverance, and being a life-long learner.

I am proud of myself for demonstrating honesty, kindness, and compassion.

I give myself permission to let go of the struggle.

I forgive myself for the mistakes I have made.

I give myself permission to appreciate and celebrate the ways I have shown up as a parent and the best parts of me that I know you have witnessed.

I give myself permission to appreciate the beautiful parts of my being.

I now release the struggle and allow myself to simply be a witness to your beautiful unfolding.

TAKING IN *and* SENDING OUT

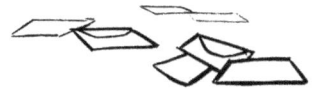

recently learned about the Tibetan Buddhist practice of Tonglen, which means, "taking in and sending out." My simple understanding is that we can acknowledge the suffering of another as we inhale (taking in), and as we exhale, we can become a conduit for sharing the boundless love and well-being that exists in the infinite space of the universe (sending out). I love the idea that we are invited to be a channel for all the goodness that exists in the great beyond.

This seems like a productive way to use my mom-worry energy, rather than meddling in or trying to solve your problems. My butting-in usually just causes tension in our relationship and brings no real solutions or relief. These habits seem to compound the anxiety for both of us. This practice, on the other hand, feels liberating. I feel a sense of expansion as opposed to the contraction that worrying about you often brings. It helps me remember that you are held by something much larger than me.

Sometimes my thinking is so small. I forget that all existence is held within a really, really big container. I recently saw pictures from NASA's new James Webb Space Telescope. I can't even wrap my mind around the photos. One of the images showed thousands of galaxies in a tiny portion of the sky. I don't even understand how big one galaxy is. Then I saw something about a reservoir floating in space with water equivalent to 140 trillion times all the water in the world's oceans. What?! For some reason, knowing that this is the container that holds us all brings me hope.

This exercise also gets me out of my own head and personal drama as I am reminded that everyone experiences feelings of insecurity, unworthiness, fear, and vulnerability. Just. Like. Me. It is a way of redirecting my attention and cultivating greater compassion towards others and myself. When I feel stuck or worried, it is an invitation to experience a much bigger picture than the one that is in my head. This calms my nervous system.

It feels like prayer to me.

Sometimes your suffering brings up fears about my own shortcomings as a parent. I'm going to breathe that in… and let it go too.

Continually flogging myself with regrets serves no one. Releasing and remembering that I am held by this vast and loving container feels gentle and healing.

I'm imagining what your internal experience is like on some of your lowest days. I acknowledge your suffering as I breathe in…

I breathe it out into the space where both of us can find healthier ways to move through uncomfortable situations without panic, despair, or damaging our relationship. I breathe it out towards all those galaxies. I release it into that space of boundless love, infinite possibility, and endless creative ways to get from here to where you want to be.

GRATITUDE *for the* STRUGGLES *and* MY LEARNER'S HEART

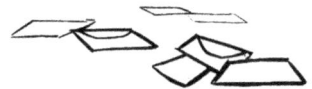

feel proud. I have always shown up even if it wasn't with my best self and even if I didn't have all the right tools.

I have shown up after mistakes.

I have shown up even when you were having a hard time being nice to me. Sometimes you even let me show up after I haven't been the nicest to you.

I feel proud. Every day, I have tried to do better.

I feel grateful. I still want to learn. I want to do better. I have a learner's heart. I pray that this quality stays with me until my last breath.

I feel grateful. Through this journey, I have learned more about what it means to be human. I have learned more about you.

Without this struggle, I'm not sure I would have grown and learned as much as I have. I hope this learning doesn't stop.

I have been working on my perspective-taking ability. More, please.

I am learning to be less rigid and more flexible. More, please.

I am learning to question my thoughts. More, please.

I am starting to learn to sit in discomfort and uncertainty. This might have been the point all along. I wish I had learned this earlier. More, please.

I am starting to learn to accept that things will always be messy. We never "arrive."

I can welcome each struggle as an opportunity to learn. I can walk into the wind and dance with life in ways I once couldn't.

The silver lining has always been that I get an opportunity to build a more authentic, human-to-human relationship with you.

For this, I say "thank you" to the struggles.

MAY YOU ALWAYS VIEW LIFE THROUGH *an* ARTIST'S EYE

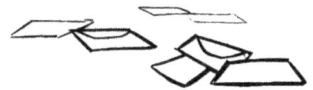

I wish for you an artist's eye. An eye that catches tiny details and celebrates the beauty of the small things, the everyday things. An eye that can view things from new angles and see elements of wonder that others might simply walk by.

May you notice the way the bubbles rise in a glass of sparkling water.

Instead of just looking at a whole flower, perhaps you will notice the way certain petals fold and curl, or the pattern in the very center, or the contrasting color of the stamen. May you recognize that one tiny piece of the flower can be a magnificent work of art, worthy of capture in a photo or simply in your mind's eye.

I hope you will notice the different ways the light plays on the hills through the changing seasons or the silhouette of a cricket sitting on a flower gone to seed against the dusky light.

Perhaps one rainy day you will be on a walk and notice the way water pouring off of a building over the mural of a face changes everything about the image. I wonder what feelings that experience will bring up in you?

I hope you won't just walk by the dew drop being cradled by a leaf. I hope you will stop and notice how it reflects the sky. Or perhaps, as you peer into that crystal clear droplet, you will notice the image of the miracle that is you reflected back.

Maybe you will notice the complex and stunning patterns in the wings of an insect or that your dog's ears are amazing and velvety soft or that your brown cat has one pinkish-white toe.

And when someone you love is standing on your last nerve, I hope you will notice something in the way they laugh or a sparkle in their eye that softens your heart and reconnects you.

When the self-critical voice tries to take you down, may you notice tiny miracles about yourself and learn to appreciate yourself just as you are in that moment. May your heart be continually softening towards yourself. You are an extraordinary gift and you are worthy of self-compassion.

It is grounding to notice things in nature. There is a softening of rough edges and a warming of the heart. You deserve this sort of grounding, softening, and warming in this sometimes noisy, sharp, and cold world. The world, this gift of life, deserves more people who are grounded.

MAYBE THIS *is* HOW HUMANS GET BETTER

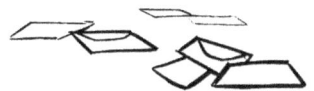

P erhaps this wasn't all for nothing.

Perhaps we have been asked to journey together as parent and child in this time and place to play an important role in the evolution of our species.

Maybe this is the point of parenting.

Maybe it did have to get really messy first. It is really, really messy right now.

I can accept this and work with it. Maybe it is the part we get to play in creating the gentle world that life has been calling out to for centuries.

But it is so hard and so, so messy. It is messy on the inside and on the outside. It is messy at the micro level and the macro level.

If this is the compost that heals and is part of an evolution, a revolution, then I can accept the compost (otherwise known as shit).

If this starts to bring generational healing and real change, I think I can take the shit.

If this is the mission, I choose to accept it.

BULLET POINTS *from the* LECTURE I WANT *to* GIVE TODAY

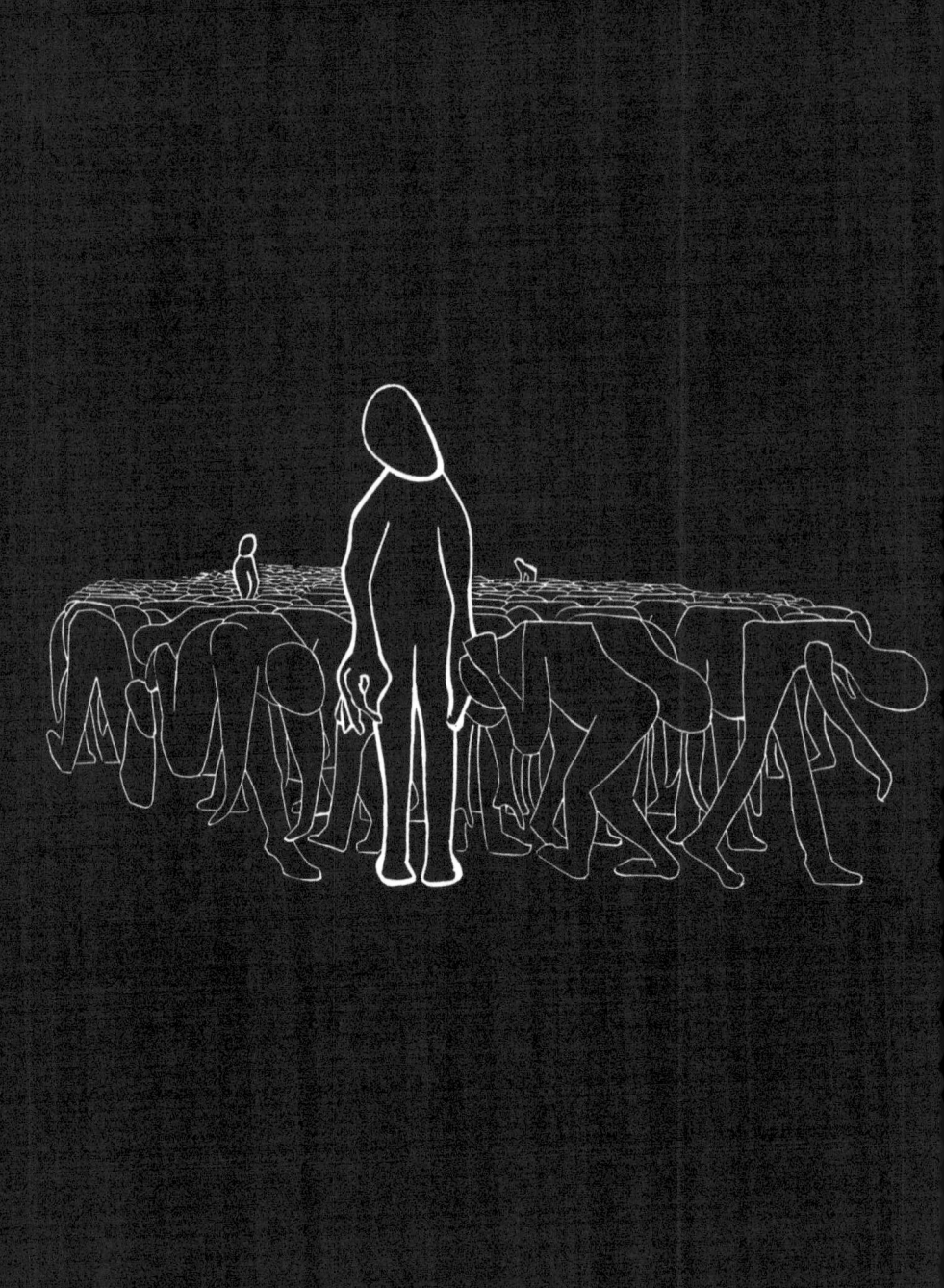

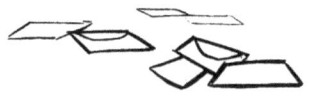

1. I hope you will soon see that you are a unique expression of life with unlimited possibilities. You are wonderful just as you are. You are enough!

2. You are worthy of a good life.

3. I know that the world seems complex and overwhelming at times, but a good life is still possible. So much is still possible.

4. You deserve good friends. I see how loyal you are to your friends. You deserve to be treated with love, kindness, and thoughtfulness by those you choose to let into your life. I hope you will surround yourself with people who can offer this to you in the same way you give it to others. This is not a comment on the friends you have. I don't know most of them. It's just something I wish for you. A couple of quotes I really like about friends include:

   > "The people you surround yourself with influence your behaviors, so choose friends who have healthy habits." —Dan Buettner

   > "Surround yourself with only people who are going to lift you higher." —-Oprah Winfrey

If this describes your current group of friends, I am thrilled for you. If there are some people that you need to walk away from, I hope you will. Another sentiment I adore is, "We have not yet met all the people who are going to love us and who we are going to love."

5. You deserve love, kindness, and thoughtfulness from yourself.

6. Part of treating yourself with loving kindness is getting into a self-care routine with your body, mind, soul, and physical space/possessions. I recently read an Instagram post that resonated: "Your entire life can change with six months of consistency. Perfection isn't the goal. Consistency is. Don't try to be perfect. Try to be better than you were yesterday. Consistency beats perfectionism."

7. I hope you can do a little something each day that your future self will thank you for.

8. A big part of life is suffering—for everyone. So I guess you could call a lot of suffering "normal life suffering." Accept that it exists but know that suffering/discomfort/negative thoughts are like clouds that come and go. Know that nothing is permanent and it will be ok. Bad moments happen. Bad days happen. Bad seasons happen. Then you get an easier season. It is a repeating cycle and how we learn and grow. You are not the clouds. You are the sky, infinite with possibility.

9. I hope that when the going gets rough, you are aware of your go-to habits for escaping/numbing out, and that you choose the healthiest possible coping mechanisms.

10. I cannot take away your struggles. I have spent a lot of years trying to problem-solve for you when you have struggled. I

thought I could fix whatever was wrong. I cannot. It never works. I can't take away depression. I can't instill motivation or grit. Whatever you generate from the inside is the only true power you have in this life. May you cultivate self-love, self-acceptance, self-care, perseverance, grit, creative thinking and problem-solving, acceptance of what is, and the will to change what you can.

11. You have grown up in a world where there is a lot of instant gratification. So much choice, literally at your fingertips. The problem is that nothing worth really having and protecting is instant. Deep relationships, mastering a skill, building a career, developing yourself—all of these take time, grit, tears and sweat. And believe me…they are worth the work. There will be many peaks, valleys, and plateaus and spending time in each can provide valuable learning.

12. We always have choices. We are never truly stuck.

13. Working towards controlling your own mind is the greatest gift you can give yourself. Remember that your thoughts are not facts and you do not have to believe every thought that visits. You get to control whether or not your thoughts imprison you. However, you will have to work at this for your entire life. You will never arrive at a place of mastery. It is an infinite journey, not a destination. It is something you can work to improve every day with every situation you face.

14. I hope you find a way to dwell in possibility. To find miracles in the ordinary. When you really think about it, nothing is ordinary. The mysterious gift of life is absolutely extraordinary.

I hope that you continually work to tap into gratitude for all the ways life has provided and continues to provide for you.

While the heavy lifting in your life is now 100% up to you, I will always be here to support you in healthy ways. I can listen and validate when things are hard. I will always express my confidence in your ability to learn your way through ANYTHING. I know you are so very capable. I love you.

Lecture concluded. Mom out.

VASHTI SUMMERVILL
Educator, Certified Parent Coach, Therapeutic Consultant and Musician

Vashti considers it her life's work to build community and connection. She is a mom, a passionate educator, and a musician. She also has firsthand experience parenting teens and young adults through very difficult times. She has embarked on a journey to combine her education and her lived experience to help support other parents, especially those struggling in their relationship with "tweens," teens, and young adults.

She has a full parent coaching and therapeutic consulting practice. She regularly tours and evaluates therapeutic programs for adolescents and young adults so she can assist parents in finding the right resources for their children.

Music continues to play a big role in her life. She has an extensive background in performance as well as teaching/directing. She continues to write music and perform regularly. She released her debut album, *Put My Love In a Picture*, in September of 2022.

Vashti is a voracious life-long learner. She received a Bachelor of Arts in Music from Colorado Mesa University in Grand Junction, Colorado and a Master's of Music/Vocal Performance from Western Washington University in Bellingham, Washington. In addition to receiving her Parent Coaching Certification from the Parent Coaching Institute, she is trained in Youth Mental Health First Aid, ASIST (Applied Suicide Intervention Skills Training), as a QPR Instructor (Suicide Prevention Gatekeeper Training), and held an Elementary Teaching certification with a K-12 Music Endorsement. Vashti is a qualified Mindfulness Based Stress Reduction Teacher (MBSR) through Brown University.

You can learn more about Vashti's work with families at
familyhealingpathways.com and **educationalconnections.com**
and more about her music at
vashtisummervill.com

WENDY BLICKENSTAFF

Artist, Educator, Activity Therapist,
Behavior Intervention Specialist,
Graduate Student in Clinical
Mental Health Counseling

Wendy Blickenstaff is an award-winning community-building artist. Examples of her installation work can be found archived online at Idaho Matters on Boise State public radio and on the Creators, Makers and Doers blog of the City of Boise Department of Arts and History. She is a recipient of a COVID Cultural Commissioning Fund grant, part of the City of Boise's Department of Arts and History's Covid Community Collection, and a Boise Open Studios Collective Organization member.

Wendy owns Blick-Studios, an art studio specializing in illustration and image design through linoleum block printing. Her images are used in mental health curricula, private art practice, and community-building projects. Through years of collaboration with local community outreach programs, Wendy has created a critical mass of images to tell our society's mental health story. Her current body of work contains over a hundred narrative images shared in various venues, from churches and homeless shelters to social justice programs and hospitals.

Wendy holds a Bachelor of Fine Arts in Printmaking from Boise State University and a Bachelor's in Studio Art from California State University, Fullerton. She is seeking a master's degree in clinical mental health counseling. She plans to expand her community-building art practice to include mental health education and counseling.

Wendy is a Boise-based artist working in her community for the common good. Her curiosity and love of novelty and diversity have inspired her to travel. You can find her most Saturdays hiking the Boise foothills or in her art studio. Her studio is often shared with other artists and friends. Wendy says, "People are our greatest resource for creating healthy communities."

You can find out more about Wendy and her art practice at
wendyblickenstaff.com or **@wendyblickenstaffart**